SHORT CIRCULAR
IN
EAST DEVON

by
JOHN N. MERRILL
(Footslogger)

Maps and photographs by John N. Merrill.

TRAIL CREST PUBLICATIONS

1992

1

New Gardens, Winster.

TRAIL CREST PUBLICATIONS Ltd.,
WINSTER, MATLOCK, DERBYSHIRE. DE4 2DQ
☎ Winster (0629) 650454
FAX Winster (0629) 650416

Edited, typeset, designed, paged, marketed and distributed by John N. Merrill.

© Text and routes - John N. Merrill 1992.

© Maps and photographs - John N. Merrill 1992.

First Published -   April 1992

ISBN 0 907496 96 2

Please note : The maps in this guide are purely illustrative. You are encouraged to walk with the appropriate Ordnance Survey map as detailed for each walk.

Meticulous research has been undertaken to ensure that this publication is highly accurate at the time of going to press. The publishers, however, cannot be held responsible for alterations, errors or omissions, but they would welcome notification of such for future editions.

Typeset in - Bookman - bold, italic and plain 9pt and 18pt.

Printed by - John N. Merrill at Milne House, Speedwell Mill, Miller's Green, Wirksworth, Derbyshire. DE4 4BL

Cover sketch - "Beer" by John Creber.
© John N. Merrill 1992.

An all British product.

CONTENTS

Page No. -

About Footslogger...4
Introduction 5
About the walks 7

COASTAL WALKS -

Axmouth to Lyme Regis - 7 1/2 miles 8
Beer & Hooken Cliffs - 7 miles 12
Branscombe and Weston Combe - 9 miles 16
Sidmouth & Salcombe Regis - 6 miles..............................20
Bulverton Hill, River Otter & Ladram Bay - 9 miles 24
Budleigh Salterton & Ladram Bay - 10 miles 28
Budleigh Salterton & Exmouth - 4, 5 & 8 miles 32
The Exeter Canal - 5 1/2 miles 36
Observe the Coastal Code 39

INLAND WALKS -

Colyton & Colyford - 1 1/2 miles 40
Colyton & Sand Pit Hill - 4 miles 42
Colyton & Shute Hill - 10 miles 46
Sidbury & White Cross - 6 miles 50
Right of Way Obstruction form 53
Broadhembury & North Hill - 6 miles 54
River Otter and Ottery St. Mary - 5 miles 58
Woodbury Common - 4 miles 60

Walk Record Chart 62
The John Merrill Walk Badge Order Form 63
Equipment Notes 64
Hiking Code...65
Country Code..66
Other books by John N. Merrill 67

Hi!
- a few notes about Footslogger.

He was born in the flatlands around Luton in Bedfordshire, but his athletic capabilities soon showed themselves on Sports Day and in the football and cricket teams. Although expelled twice from different schools, he moved to Sheffield and was taken out into the Peak District at the age of 6 1/2. Here he ran up and down the rocks and the sense of enjoyment and freedom has never left him. He was hooked on the outdoors for life. By the age of 15 he had 350 books on the Himalayas and other mountain areas and although failed all eight O levels, he was writing a book on the history of mountaineering! At 16 he soloed the 90 foot high school building and the headmaster rushed him off to Outward Bound Mountain School to be properly trained - he thought it was a fantastic holiday!

At 17 he was chosen with eleven others to go on an expedition to Norway, for a month. Since then he has walked more than 150,000 miles in different parts of the world. He has walked The Cleveland Way 8 times; The Peakland Way 14 times; The Limey Way 14 times; The Pennine Way 4 times; Offa's Dyke 3 times; Pembrokeshire Coast Path 3 times; and all the other official paths at least twice.

He is an avid walker and never known to be really tired; likes to carry heavy loads at 18,000 feet and hates having his socks or shirts washed after a six month walk! His ideal day is a 25 mile walk with three bars of chocolate in his pocket. Having worn out over fifty pairs of boots he truly lives upto his nickname, Footslogger!

INTRODUCTION

On my walk around the entire coastline of Britain in 1978 - the first person to do so - 7,000 miles in ten months! - I have very fond memories of the East Devon coast. Although it was late January the weather was fine, I walked from Lyme Regis to Exmouth in a day, but as it grew dark I neared Budleigh Salterton and was met on the cliffs and had a companion for the final miles to Exmouth. As a result I didn't see the spectacular coastline, especially Ladram Bay. As I walked my parents moved from the Peak District to Budleigh Salterton, where they retired. Consequently, I became a frequent visitor and began exploring the coast and inland country.

Here then are some of the fruits of my wandering! The whole of the coast from Lyme Regis to Exmouth in stages, in the form of circular walks. Inland the walks take you into the rolling countryside, past thatched cottages and majestic heights. One walk explores the Exeter Canal, which is steeped in history, and you can take a ferry to the start.

I have enjoyed immensely wandering the cliffs, seeing the landslips, golden beaches, watching the wildlife or gulls soaring. Inland the walking is quieter and fewer people. Here you can relax by a hedge and listen to a buzzard overhead or wander down a river and see a kingfisher. I have many favourites; the Otter Valley being one. Ladram Bay and its rock stacks are another. Branscombe Mouth and its landslip are another. Inland I fell in love Colyton, a most attractive village. Broadhembury is outstanding, and walking across Woodbury Common is a delight.

May I wish you "Happy walking" as you walk these walks. I am now walking in South Devon for the next book!

Happy walking!

John N. Merrill
Budleigh Salterton.

View to Sidmouth from Windgate near High Peak.

River Otter north of Colaton Raleigh.

ABOUT THE WALKS

Whilst every care is taken detailing and describing the walk in this book, it should be borne in mind that the countryside changes by the seasons and the work of man. I have described the walk to the best of my ability, detailing what I have found on the walk in the way of stiles and signs. Obviously with the passage of time stiles become broken or replaced by a ladder stile or even a small gate. Signs too have a habit of being broken or pushed over. All the route follow rights of way and only on rare occasions will you have to overcome obstacles in its path, such as a barbed wire fence or electric fence. On rare occasions rights of way are rerouted and these ammendments are included in the next edition.

The seasons bring occasional problems whilst out walking which should also be borne in mind. In the height of summer paths become overgrown and you will have to fight your way through in a few places. In low lying areas the fields are often full of crops, and although the pathline goes straight across it may be more practical to walk round the field edge to get to the next stile or gate. In summer the ground is generally dry but in autumn and winter, especially because of our climate, the surface can be decidedly wet and slippery; sometimes even gluttonous mud!

These comments are part of countryside walking which help to make your walk more interesting or briefly frustrating. Standing in a farmyard up to your ankles in mud might not be funny at the time but upon reflection was one of the highlights of the walk!

The mileage for each walk is based on three calculations -

1. pedometer reading.
2. the route map measured on the map.
3. the time I took for the walk.

I believe the figure stated for each walk to be very accurate but we all walk differently and not always in a straight line! The time allowed for each walk is on the generous side and does not include pub stops etc. The figure is based on the fact that on average a person walks 2 1/2 miles an hours but less in hilly terrain.

AXMOUTH/LYME REGIS UNDERCLIFFS - 7 1/2 MILES

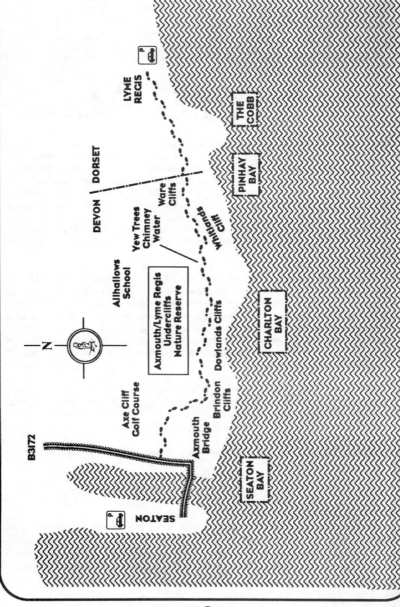

8

AXMOUTH to LYME REGIS via UNDERCLIFFS
- 7 1/2 MILES
- allow 3 1/2 hours.

•• •• •• •• *- Axmouth Bridge - Axe Cliff Golf Course - Coast Path - Axmouth/Lyme Regis Undercliffs Nature Reserve - Bindon Cliffs - Dowlands Cliffs - Charlton Bay - Whitlands Cliff - Pinhay Cliffs - Ware Cliffs - The Cobb - Lyme Regis.*

1:25,000 Pathfinder Series Sheet No. SY 29/39 - Lyme Regis and Axminster.

- In Seaton and small parking area at the start beside the Golf Course road and B3172 road at Grid Ref: SY254902.

- None on the walk but several in Seaton and Lyme Regis.

ABOUT THE WALK - The coastal path between Axmouth Bridge and Lyme Regis is some of the hardest and remotest section of coastal walking in Southern England. Between the two places there is no right of way to the sea or inland. As a result you cannot do a circular walk. The best alternative and one way to enjoy and experience this remote and wild stretch is to walk to Charlton Bay - about half way - and return the same way. If you can be met at Lyme Regis or catch a bus back to Seaton then it makes a really splendid end to end walk. I have started from the Devon end (Axmouth Bridge) as I primarily wanted to concentrate within the boundaries of Devon - Lyme Regis is just over the border in Dorset! The walk is spectacular with many landslips, heavy woodland - usually impenetrable , and a wide variety of birds, flowers and ferns.

WALKING INSTRUCTIONS - From Axmouth Bridge, follow the coastal path sign and ascend the tarmaced drive to the car park and club house of the Axe Cliff Golf Club. Walk past the buildings on your right and watching out for golf balls ascend straight ahead guided by signs to a stile and hedged track. Continue ascending gently for another 1/4 mile the path sign and track on your right. The notice tells you about the terrain ahead - difficult and arduous and about 3

9

1/2 hours to Lyme Regis. Turn right along the track to its end and a stile. The path is well defined as you keep to the field edge and bear left to the top of the cliffs and entrance into the Nature Reserve 1/2 mile away. Here you descend steps and enter the woodland and cliffs. The path weaves around with several ascents and descents and in about an hour you should reach Charlton Bay; although you see little of it. The area is recognisable by the sudden change from a small path to a wide drive with several yew trees on your left. Just beyond is a bridge with metal railings, a solitary chimney, and water ponds. Here you have to decide either to continue to Lyme Regis - 1 1/2 hours away - or retrace your steps back to Axmouth Bridge.

If starting from Lyme Regis -

Car Park - Holmbush, through which the coastal path passes. Or alternatively on The Cobb where a signed path leads to the coast path. The walk from here along the coast path is excellent passing Ware Cliffs and around Pinhay Bay and on past Whitlands Cliff to Charlton Bay. Here you can return to Lyme Regis or continue on to Seaton.

Coast Path warning notice.

Seaton Bay.

The Cobb, Lyme Regis.

BEER & HOOKEN CLIFFS
- 7 MILES

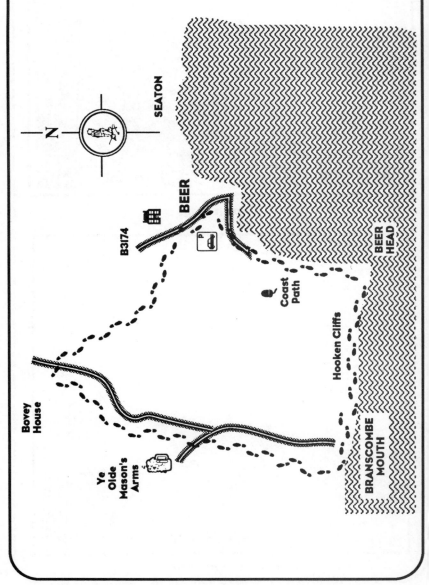

SEATON

N

BEER

B3174

Coast Path

BEER HEAD

Hooken Cliffs

Bovey House

Ye Olde Mason's Arms

BRANSCOMBE MOUTH

BEER & HOOKEN CLIFFS - 7 MILES

- allow 2 1/2 hours

- ● ● ● ● **-** *Beer - Beer Head - Under Hooken Cliffs - Branscombe Mouth - Vicarage (Branscombe) - Bovey House - Beer.*

- *1:25,000 Pathfinder Sheet No. SY29/39 - Lyme Regis and Axminster.*

 - Central Beer and Branscombe Mouth.

- Beer - Dolphin Inn, Barrel of Beer Inn, and Anchor Inn. Vicarage (Branscombe) - Ye Olde Masons Arms.

ABOUT THE WALK - You can start the walk from either Beer or Branscombe Mouth. The scenery is stunning with the Hooken Cliffs a magnificent landslip. You walk inland to Vicarage and its beautiful thatched inn before following lanes to the entrance drive to the 16th Century hotel - Bovey House. Here you descend through woodland back to Beer and the sea. A splendid circuit and one that I never tire of walking!

WALKING INSTRUCTIONS - Starting from Beer - gain the main road and turn right passing the Barrel of Beer Inn and the Anchor Inn. Follow the road - Common Lane - round to your right and in a short distance turn left at the coast path sign onto Little Lane - "Branscombe Mouth 1 3/4 miles." You soon pass caravans on your right as the lane turns sharp left and you begin ascending gently, now on a path heading for the summit of Beer Head 1/2 mile away. Follow the cliff top around to your right for a short distance to a stile and footpath sign - Branscombe 1 mile. Turn left and follow the well defined path down into the middle of the landslip - Under Hooken. The path is superb walking! Keep on this path for almost a mile and as you near Branscombe Mouth you pass many holiday chalets nestling on the broken ground. Join the track to them and cross a cattle grid and bear left and descend to Branscombe Mouth and its car park.

Keep to the coast side and pass the thatched shop on your right. Just after turn right on a track and in 150 yards reach a footbridge. Cross this and follow the path around to your left passing Little Seaside on your right. Continue along the field edge to more footbridges and turn right to reach the houses of Vicarage and the Ye Olde Masons Arms on your left. Cross the road diagonally to your right and follow Beer Road for the next 3/4 mile - a 1 in 6 hill. Ignore the first turning on your left but take the next one 1/4 mile later. The lane descends and ascends to the entrance drive of Bovey House Hotel. Opposite turn right, as bridlepath signed, and follow the track which gradually descends through delightful woodland and in a mile reach the fringe of Beer, with the Youth Hostel on your left and the Grange, and a garage a little to your right. Keep straight ahead along Townsend road which soon becomes the Causeway. At the road junction keep right and pass a 16th Century Manor House before bearing right again at the Public Convience to reach central Beer, the Dolphin Inn and car park just off to your right.

Hooken Cliffs.

Bovey House.

Ye Olde Masons Arms, Vicarage, Branscombe.

15

BRANSCOMBE AND WESTON COMBE - 9 MILES

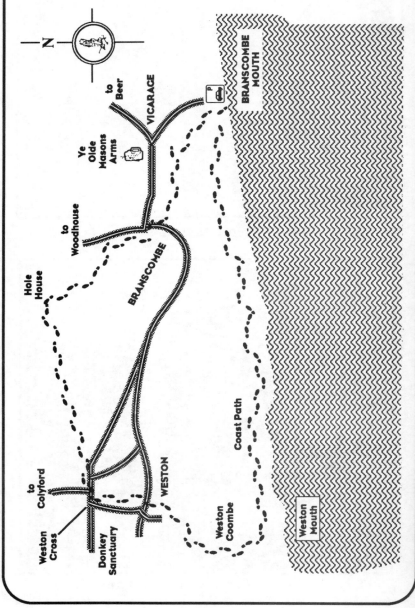

BRANSCOMBE & WESTON COMBE - 9 MILES

- allow 3 1/2 hours.

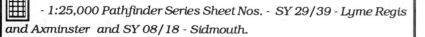 *- Branscombe Mouth - Branscombe - Hole House - Hole Hill - Ashton - Weston Cross - Weston - Weston Combe - Coast Path - Weston Cliff - Branscombe Mouth.*

O.S. MAP *- 1:25,000 Pathfinder Series Sheet Nos. - SY 29/39 - Lyme Regis and Axminster and SY 08/18 - Sidmouth.*

- Branscombe Mouth. Grid Ref: SY208882.

- None actually on the walk, the nearest is at Vicarage (Branscombe) just off the route - "Ye Olde Masons Arms."

ABOUT THE WALK - The coastal scenery at Branscombe Mouth is outstanding. This walk takes you inland first to the attractive village of Branscombe before follow sunken lanes to Weston. Here you can continue a little further - adding a mile extra to the walk - and visit the Donkey Sanctuary. You descend Weston Combe to the cliff tops and follow the coastal path back to Branscombe Mouth, getting superlative views of the Hooken Cliffs and its landslip.

WALKING INSTRUCTIONS - From the car park at Branscombe Mouth walk towards the shore and turn right along the path past the thatched shop. Turn right immediately afterwards onto a track and follow this to a footbridge. Cross this and follow the path round to your left, passing Little Seaside on your right. Keep to the field edge to some footbridges and path to your right - this leads to Vicarage village and the Ye Olde Masons Arms. Follow the path to your left which in 1/4 mile reaches the village of Branscombe, by the path sign - "Branscombe Mouth." Basically cross the road and begin ascending the road opposite, with the village hall and The Forge on your left. Ascend the road for 1/4 mile and just past the house called - Hobble - turn left through a gate. This right of way is little used. Descend the field aiming for the base of the shallow valley where there is a footbridge. Cross this and turn right; the pathline is non existent and you are walking in woodland which is often quite wet underfoot - this is only bad section on the walk. Keep near the field edge and reach a gate by a minor road.

Turn left and ascend the road past Hole House. At the junction above it, and as bridlepath signed, turn right and follow the track though a delightful sunken lane through the woodland of Hole Hill. At the end gain a hedged track; turn right along this with an airfield on your left. In 1/2 mile cross a minor road from Higher Bulstone Farm and continue on the hedged track. Follow this to its end and junction with a minor road. Continue ahead along this passing Ashton on your right. Ignore the turning on your left and the one on your right, but the next on your left at Weston Cross turn left into the village.

If you want to visit the Donkey Sanctuary continue ahead at Weston Cross. At the sanctuary - Slade House Farm - turn left onto the Weston Road and in a few yards leave the road on your right onto the path down Dunscombe to Weston Mouth; here you turn left and join the coast path back to Branscombe Mouth.

Follow the road round through Weston village and on the lefthand bend leave it, as footpath signed - "Weston Mouth 3/4 mile". There is a small car park here. Follow the track through the woodland and in just over 1/4 mile bear left and maintain height as you keep well up the side of Weston Combe and in 1/3 mile gain the coast path and turn left. The path is well stiled and signed as you ascend over Weston Cliff and onto Coxe's Cliff; here as path signed -"Branscombe Mouth 2 1/4 miles" - you walk inland to avoid the rugged coastline and in just over a mile gain a track and woodland above Branscombe. Continue on the signed coast path and soon descend West Cliff down to Branscombe Mouth.

Weston Combe and coast.

Branscombe Mouth and Hooken Cliffs.

19

SIDMOUTH & SALCOMBE
REGIS - 6 MILES

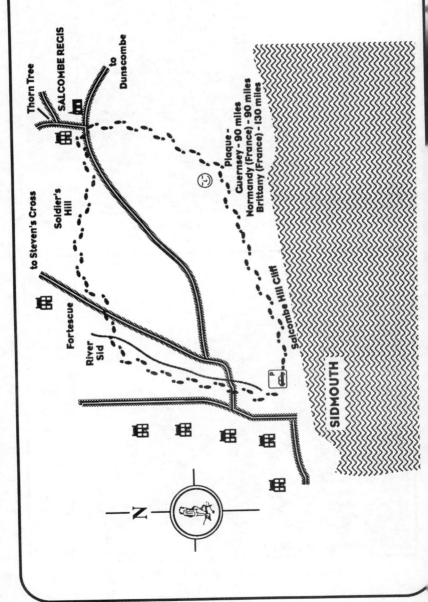

Thorn Tree

SALCOMBE REGIS

to Dunscombe

to Steven's Cross

Soldier's Hill

Plaque -
Guernsey - 90 miles
Normandy (France) - 90 miles
Brittany (France) - 130 miles

Fortescue

River Sid

Salcombe Hill Cliff

SIDMOUTH

N

SIDMOUTH & SALCOMBE REGIS
- 6 MILES

- allow 2 1/4 hours

 - Sidmouth - Coast Path - Salcombe Hill - Salcombe Regis - Soldier's Hill - Fortescue - The Byes - River Sid - Sidmouth.

 - 1:25,000 Pathfinder Series Sheet No. SY 08/18 - Sidmouth.

 - Sidmouth, near the shore at Grid Ref. SY128874.

- Numerous in Sidmouth - at the end of the walk!

ABOUT THE WALK - Salcombe Hill is an impressive vantage point with France on the horizon. From here you walk inland to the attractive historical village of Salcombe Regis. Just off the route is the Salcombe Regis Thorn tree marking the boundary of common and cultivated fields, dating back to Saxon times. You return over a hill and descend to the River Sid which you follow back into Sidmouth. A really delightful short walk!

WALKING INSTRUCTIONS - From the car park in Sidmouth walk towards the sea front and turn left and cross the bridge over the River Sid and ascend the coast path. The path is well defined and leads you close to the cliff edge as you ascend Salcombe Hill, National Trust property. On its summit is a circular directional plaque, pointing to where Guernsey 90 miles; Normandy (France) 90 miles; and Brittany (France) 130 miles away. Continue along the summit plateau and where the path descends towards Salcombe Mouth 1/2 mile away, turn left along the field edge to a gate and onto another. Shortly after at the entrance to woodland gain the footpath sign - "Salcombe Regis - 1/2 mile". Follow the track down through the woodland and in 1/3 mile gain a minor road by a Sidmouth path sign. Turn left to Salcombe Regis church - well worth looking round.

Opposite the church turn left and ascend Sidmouth Road to a war memorial at the road junction. Cross the road to a stile and follow the path across the James Cornish Field over Soldier Hill. Reach a stile and descend slightly to the next. Here you descend more steeply to a lane and continue ahead - signed footpath to "Griggs Lane". You soon enter Griggs Lane and the houses of Fortescue. At the road junction turn left and in a few yards turn right, as path signed - "The Byes" and descend to the footbridge over the River Sid. Cross this to The Byes footpath where turn left. For the final 1 1/2 miles back to the car park at Sidmouth you keep close to the River Sid. After 1/4 mile it is on your left and into Sid Meadows (National Trust property) cross over so it is on your right. 1/2 mile later gain a road and the sea is now 548 metres away. Turn right then left along Riverside Road which will bring you back to the car park.

Salcombe Regis church.

The Salcombe Regis Thorn.

23

BULVERTON HILL, RIVER OTTER & LADRAM BAY - 9 MILES

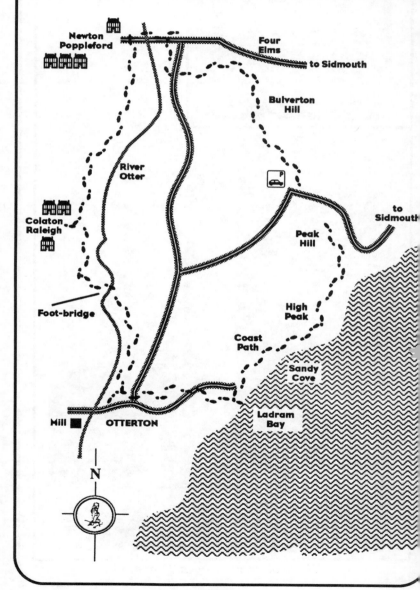

BULVERTON HILL, RIVER OTTER AND LADRAM BAY - 9 MILES

- allow 3 1/2 hours.

- Peak Hill Car Park - Mutter's Moor - Bulverton Hill - Four Elms - Northmostown - Newton Poppleford - River Otter - Colaton Raleigh - River Otter - Otterton - Ladram Bay - Coast Path - High Peak - Peak Hill Car Park.

 - 1:25,000 Pathfinder Series Sheet No. SY 08/18 - Sidmouth.

- and start - Peak Hill Car Park at Grid Ref. SY109873.

- King's Arms, Otterton; Three Rocks Inn, Ladram Bay (in season); others off the route in Newton Poppleford and Colaton Raleigh.

ABOUT THE WALK - An outstanding walk combing a mixture of East Devon walking. Firstly through woodland before descending to the River Otter which you follow to the attractive thatched village of Otterton. From here you make your way to the coast and the spectacular rock stacks. You ascend over High Peak back to Peak Hill. This is one walk that I never tire of walking whatever the season.

WALKING INSTRUCTIONS - From the car park follow the bridleway out it - a track - signposted Bulverton Hill 1 1/4 miles. The level track for the next 3/4 mile keeps to the edge of Mutter's Moor - an extensive lowland heath - on your left and the trees of Greystone Hill Plantation on your right. Follow the blue bridleway signs for Bulverton Hill and where the track divides keep to the righthand one. Nearly 1 1/2 miles from the car park gain the cross roads of paths/tracks close to Kebells Seat. Turn left and descend the track signposted - Back Lane, Four Elms, 1/2 mile. Just before the road at Four Elms turn left along another track which swings to your left then right and becomes a delightful sunken lane as you descend to the hamlet of Northmostown.

Turn right along the road with the River Otter below you on your left. At the junction with the A3052 Sidmouth road turn left and cross the River Otter and enter Newton Poppleford.

Take the first road on your left - Millmoor Lane - and where it turns left keep straight ahead to a gate and footpath sign - Colaton Raleigh 1 1/2 miles - on the right of Harley Cottage. The path is tarmaced at first but soon becomes just a path on the lefthand edge of the fields. For nearly 1/2 mile you are away from the river but you are soon beside it for a short distance before gaining the track near Dotton Farm. Turn left then right at a kissing gate, and continue towards Colaton Raleigh, now a mile away. The pathline is faint across the middle of the narrow field but reach a stile at the other end and ascend the track to your left to the top of an impressive sandstone cliff. Continue along the defined path with the hedge on your right and cross two stiles before gaining a hedged track. Continue along this to Colaton Raleigh.

Gaining the road turn left and in a few yards at the end of the road go through a kissing gate. Keep to the lefthand side of the field to the river where turn right and keep the river on your left for more than 1/2 mile to a large curving wooden footbridge over the river. Turn left and cross the bridge and turn right walking high above the river. The path is well defined and in less 1/2 mile you descend to Otterton. To your right is Otterton Mill. Turn left along the road through the village along Fore Street and past the King's Arms. At the road junction later follow Bell Street, signposted Ladram Bay 1 mile. Ascend the road and a 1/3 mile turn right along a track footpath signposted - Ladram Bay 3/4 mile. In a few yards turn left and follow the hedged track as it weaves way round the caravan complex at Ladram Bay. Gaining the road there turn right and in a few yards left, now joining the coast path signposted - Sidmouth 2 1/4 miles.

The path passes the Three Rocks Inn on your left and beyond you gain a stile. Continue along the top of the cliffs, now beginning to ascend. On your right is Ladram Bay and its rock stacks. Ascend to a stile and steps and enter the pine trees around High Peak. Continue ascending through the trees on a wide path, which soon levels out as you keep well to the left of the hill top. Continue on the coast path close to the cliffs again around "Windgate". Gaining another stile you begin ascending again towards Peak Hill. The coast path goes to your right but take the lefthand grass track which is more gentle. On the top bear left and head towards the carpark where you began.

The coast around Ladram Bay.

Rock Stacks, Ladram Bay.

BUDLEIGH SALTERTON & LADRAM BAY - 10 MILES

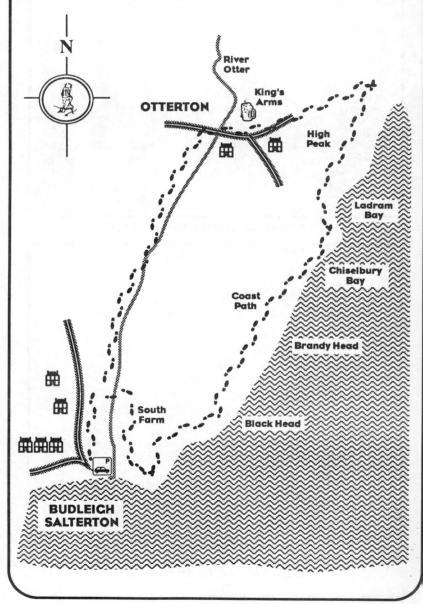

N

River Otter

King's Arms

OTTERTON

High Peak

Ladram Bay

Chiselbury Bay

Coast Path

Brandy Head

South Farm

Black Head

BUDLEIGH SALTERTON

BUDLEIGH SALTERTON & LADRAM BAY
- 10 MILES
- allow 4 hours.

■● ■● ■● ■● - Budleigh Salterton - River Otter - South Farm - Coast Path - Ladram Bay - High Peak - Sidmouth Road - Bar Lane - Otterton - River Otter - Budleigh Salterton.

 - 1:25,000 Pathfinder Series Sheet No. SY 08/18 - Sidmouth.

- Beside River Otter on east side of Budleigh Salterton. Grid Ref. SY074820.

There is also a car park on the minor road between Otterton and Sidmouth near Peak Hill at Grid Ref. SY109874.

- Numerous in Budleigh Salterton. King's Arms in Otterton. Three Rocks Inn at Ladram Bay - summer only.

ABOUT THE WALK - The walk encompasses a splendid section of coastline with rock stacks at Ladram Bay and wooded slopes of High Peak. You return via the attractive village of Otterton where you can visit the working mill before walking beside the river Otter back to Budleigh Salterton.

The walk can be extended or used a one way walk of about 7 miles to Sidmouth.

WALKING INSTRUCTIONS - Leave the car park at the north western corner where there is a well defined path. Although you can see the coast path nearby you have walk around the Otter's estuary to cross it before gaining the coast. Follow the path a short distance before turning right and following another with the playing field on your left. This path brings you close to the River Otter and in 1/2 mile gain the road bridge over it. Turn right and cross the bridge and a few yards beyond turn right and right again to follow the coast path that passes along the top of the cliffs with South Farm on your left. In just over 1/2 mile reach the cliffs and sea below - the car park is only 1/4 mile away! But, the views of Budleigh Salterton and its red cliffs make the effort worth it!

The path swings left and you ascend and now follow the defined path along the top of the cliffs. For more than 2 miles you keep on the cliffs before moving inland slightly around Ladram Bay and its caravan site. Reaching the track at the bay turn right then left to pass the Three Rocks Inn and continue along the cliffs heading for the ascent of the wooded slopes of High Peak 1/2 mile away. At the end of the woodland reach Bar Lane and path sign. Here turn left for Otterton.

If you want to continue to Sidmouth or reach the summit of Peak Hill and enjoy the view down to Sidmouth, continue along the coast path and retrace your steps later.

Follow the hedged Bar Lane for 3/4 mile to Sea View Farm and minor road. Continue ahead - the road to your left goes to Ladram Bay - ignore all branch roads and keep ahead to Otterton and pass the King's Arms Inn. Follow the road past Otterton Mill on your left and cross the River Otter. Immediately afterwards turn left onto the path by the river; signed - "Budleigh Salterton 2 miles." Keep on this path back to the car park with the river on your left. In 1 1/2 mile gain the road you used at the start and cross it and retrace you steps back to the car park.

The mouth of the River Otter and Budleigh Salterton.

Red cliffs near Budleigh Salterton.

Coast path - view to Ladram Bay and Sidmouth.

BUDLEIGH SALTERTON & EXMOUTH
- 4, 5 & 8 MILES

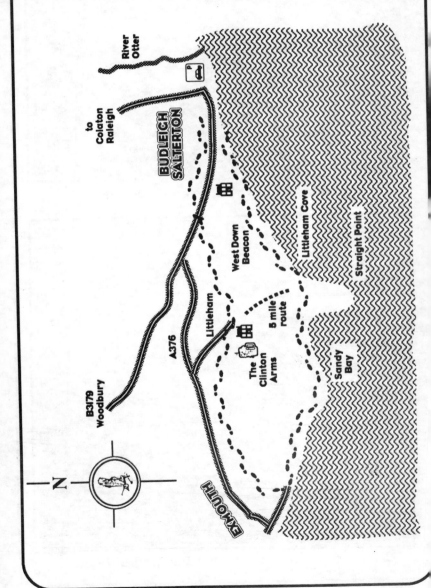

River Otter

to Colaton Raleigh

BUDLEIGH SALTERTON

Littleham Cove

Straight Point

West Down Beacon

Littleham

5 mile route

Sandy Bay

B3179 Woodbury

A376

The Clinton Arms

N

EXMOUTH

32

BUDLEIGH SALTERTON & EXMOUTH
- 4, 5 & 8 MILES
- allow 1 1/2, 2 and 3 hours.

-8 mile route - Budleigh Salterton - Coast Path - West Down Beacon - The Floors - Littleham Cove - Sandy Bay - High Land of Orcombe - The Maer - Green Farm - Littleham - Castle Lane - West Down - Golf Course - Budleigh Salterton.

- 4 mile route - Budleigh Salterton to Exmouth via the Coast Path.

- 5 mile route - from Littleham Cove - west Down Farm and road to Littleham, picking up main route here.

- 1:25,000 Pathfinder Series Sheet No. SY 08/18 - Sidmouth.

- Budleigh Salterton and Exmouth.

- Numerous in Budleigh Salterton and Exmouth. The Clinton Arms, Littleham. Tea rooms in season at Sandy Bay and Littleham.

ABOUT THE WALK- The coastal path from Budleigh Salterton to Exmouth is dramatic with many excellent views back to Budleigh and Sidmouth and southwards to the River Exe and Dawlish. The walk has three options. Either walk the coast path end to end and catch a bus back; or walk the entire circular route; or reduce it by following the path to Littleham from Littleham Cove. All three are very scenic.

WALKING INSTRUCTIONS - Starting from Budleigh Salterton walk along the road by the beach and boats and where it turns right keep ahead on the coastal footpath. The climbs gently up past houses on your right and impressive views behind of the mouth of the River Otter. The path levels off and keeps near the cliffs with a common on your right. Soon afterwards pass the East Devon Golf Club on your right - you cross it later - and continue on the wide path/track, past pine trees to the summit of West Down Beacon - 425 feet. The trig point is just to your right. You now descend and ahead can be seen Littleham Cove and large caravan site with Straight Point Rifle Range. Continue on the path as it descends above the cliffs of The Floors, to a small stream, crossed by a footbridge, and reach via stiles and steps. Ascend the field edge to the stile and perimeter of the caravan site. Continue along the coast side past the caravans and reach the path junction and sign - Littleham 1/2 mile.

- if doing the shorter walk, turn right here and walk beside the hedge and ascend to West Down Farm. Here keep ahead on the road and descend to Littleham with the Tythe Cottage Tea Room and Clinton Arms round to your right. You pick up the longer route just beyond the inn at the road junction beside the church. Near the farm you pass the "World of Country Life", which has farmyard animals and depicts rural life from 1750 to 1950.

Continue on the coast path past the entrance to Littleham Cove and Otter Cove and ascend to the perimeter fence of the Royal Marines rifle range. Continue and soon descend to Sandy Bay, keeping to the coast side, and aiming for the lefthand side of the restaurant. Keep on the coast path ascending to the National Trust property - High Land of Orcombe. Descend the otherside with views of the River Exe and Exmouth. Don't descend to the shore road but keep ahead on the path along the cliffs to a road junction. Here is walking end to end walk along the shore road into Exmouth. If not, continue ahead along Maer Road following round to your right to its junction with Douglas Avenue.

Here turn right passing The Devon Court Hotel on your right and 1/4 mile later, just past Haldon Court, bear right opposite Mayfield Drive, along the footpath signed - Littleham 1 mile. Don"t follow the path that descends to your right, but keep along the level path along an old hedged lane. At the end is a kissing gate and the whole route to Littleham has these metal kissing gate. Cross a field aiming for the righthand side of Green Farm. Continue guided by the defined path and kissing gates entering Littleham past the school on your left with a large wooden owl. Join a small road to the Post Office and turn right with the church dedicated to St. Margaret and St. Andrew on your left.

Descend the road and turn left at the bottom along Castle Lane - to your right is the Clinton Arms, where the shorter route joins the main route. Walk along Castle Lane and in 1/4 mile pass Castle Cottage on your right. A 1/3 mile later opposite Cherry Tree Cottage, turn right at the stile and path sign and follow a well defined track through Knowle Hill Plantation. Where the track turns left keep ahead to a stile and follow a path through the trees to the golf course. Cross to a track and bear left along it and where it turns left in 60 yards, follow round and bear right immediately. Cross another golf fairway to a stile and continue on a defined path across West Down and in 1/2 mile reach the Budleigh Salterton road beside Church Path House. The path you have been following is the Littleham Church Path. Turn right along the road and descend West Hill back into central Budleigh and past the shops regain the coast where you began.

The Floors and view to Budleigh Salterton.

View from West Down Beacon to Straight Point.

EXETER CANAL - 5 1/2 MILES

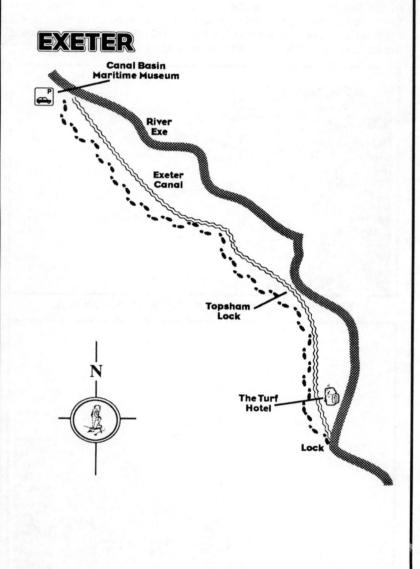

EXETER

Canal Basin
Maritime Museum

River
Exe

Exeter
Canal

Topsham
Lock

N

The Turf
Hotel

Lock

THE EXETER CANAL
- 5 1/2 MILES
- one way - allow 2 hours.

- Exeter Canal Basin - Exeter Canal to Turf Hotel and lock. Return same way.

- 1:25,000 Pathfinder Series Sheet Nos. SX 89/99 - Exeter and SX 88/98 - Great Haldon.

- Close to Exeter Canal basin, just off Haven Road. Follow signs for Maritime Museum from the Exe Bridge.

- Numerous in Exeter. Welcome Inn close to start of the canal and the Turf Hotel at the other end.

ABOUT THE WALK - A superb short canal walk with views of the River Exe and sea. You can start the walk from Exmouth by taking the ferry across from there - check times. They often run an evening boat to the Turf Hotel during the summer months; again check times. During the summer the "Water Mongoose" boat travels between Countess Wear and the Turf Hotel and could be used for your return, but check times first.

WALKING INSTRUCTIONS - The walk begins at the canal basin and basically keeps to the towpath on the western side of the canal. It is well used and signed. From the Maritime Museum - where you get a handy leaflet on the canal's history - you will have to road walk adjacent to it to get to the towpath. En route you pass swing bridges, see canoeists on the canal, and pass the abandoned Topsham lock.

EXETER CANAL - was started in the 1560's, but it wasn't until 1701 that a 10 foot deep by 50 foot wide canal was made from near Topsham lock to Exeter. In 1825 is was extended to Turf Lock, near the Hotel. Like all canals the coming of the railway saw its decline and is today solely used by pleasure boats. The canal basin - 18 feet deep by 900 feet long was built in the 1830. The Maritime Museum is well worth visiting.

Exeter Canal Basin.

Turf Hotel & Exeter Canal.

OBSERVE THE COASTAL CODE -

 PLEASE DO NOT DAMAGE SALT MARSHES, SAND DUNES AND "CLIFF TOPS" BY TRAMPLING, OR MOVING ROCKS.

 ALWAYS "BACK FILL" HOLES WHEN BAIT DIGGING AS THESE MAY BE A DANGER TO OTHERS.

 MAKE YOUR VISIT INSTRUCTIVE BY PLANNING FIELD TRIPS CAREFULLY WITH CONSERVATION IN MIND.

 TAKE PHOTOGRAPHS NOT LIVE SPECIMENS.

 PLEASE DO NOT COLLECT LIVE ANIMALS OR SEAWEEDS, LEAVE THEM FOR OTHERS TO ENJOY.

 THE COAST IS HOME FOR MANY PLANTS AND ANIMALS AND THEY MAY BE DESTROYED BY OUR CARELESS ACTIONS.

COLYFORD TO COLYTON
- 1 1/2 MILES

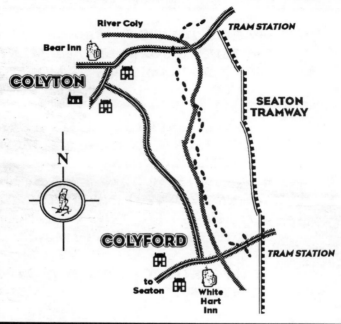

Seaton Tram at Colyford Tram Station.

COLYFORD
TO COLYTON
- 1 1/2 MILES

- allow 40 minutes.

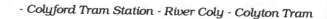 - *Colyford Tram Station - River Coly - Colyton Tram Station.*

 - *1:25,000 Pathfinder Series Sheet No. SY 29/39 - Lyme Regis and Axminster.*

 - *White Hart, Colyford; Bear Inn, The Gerrard Arms and Colocombe Castle Hotel in Colyton.*

ABOUT THE WALK - The shortest walk in the book but one of the most unusual! The idea of this short stroll is to use the Seaton Tramway either starting from Seaton and getting off at Colyford or walking from Colyford to Colyton and catching the tram back. You will need to check the times of the tram - there is a frequent service from Good Friday to the end of October. During the winter months - November to April - there is a limited service. The tram traverses part of the Axe and Coly river valleys and is the only open-top narrow gauge double decker tram operating a daily service in Britain. There is car parking in Colyton - Dolphin Street and Station and in Seaton - Harbour Road.

WALKING INSTRUCTIONS - Starting from Colyford leave the tram at the station and gain the minor road close to the White Hart Inn. Opposite is the path sign. Turn right and walk along the banks of the River Coly on your left. The path passes through a kissing gate after 1/4 mile and under a pipe before passing Giles Mill on your left. Don't cross the bridge just after but keep to the bankside and in 1/4 mile pass through another kissing gate. In a further 1/4 mile cross the river via Ham Bridge - a wooden footbridge and turn right with the river now on your right. Walk past the houses at the end to reach the road on the east side of Colyton. Turn left to explore the village and right to gain the tramway station and your return ride. Colyton is an exceptional village and well worth exploring - the church, the houses, the market place and......cream teas!

COLYTON & SAND PIT HILL - 4 MILES

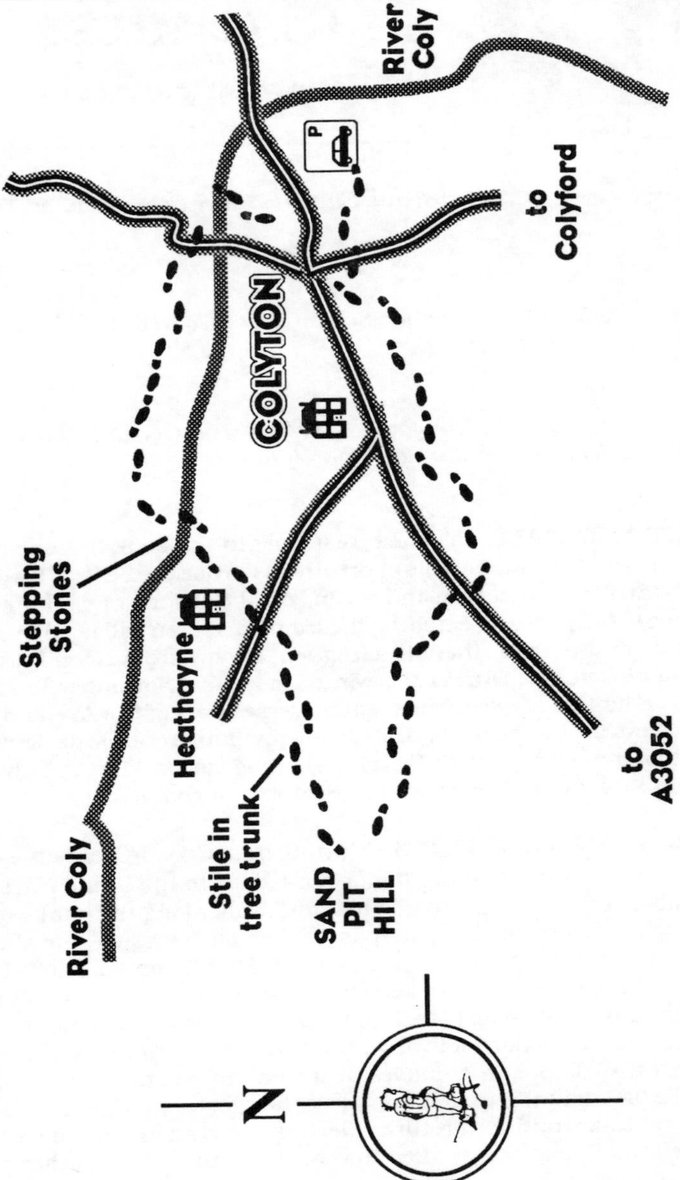

River Coly

to Colyford

COLYTON

Stepping Stones

Heathayne

Stile in tree trunk

SAND PIT HILL

River Coly

to A3052

N

COLYTON &
SAND PIT HILL
- 4 MILES

- allow 1 1/2 hours.

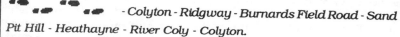 - *Colyton - Ridgway - Burnards Field Road - Sand Pit Hill - Heathayne - River Coly - Colyton.*

 - *1:25,000 Pathfinder Series Sheet No. SY 29/39 - Lyme Regis and Axminster.*

 - *off Dolphin Street in Colyton.*

 - *Bear Inn, The Gerrard Arms, Colocombe Castle Hotel, all in Colyton.*

ABOUT THE WALK - Colyton is an exceptional village and well worth exploring - its numerous historical buildings, stunning church, Market Place, and tannery etc., Little wonder it has often won the best village competition. This short walk encircles the area illustrating its great beauty. First you ascend to Sand Pit Hill with views down the Axe valley to Seaton and Axmouth before descending past a thatched house to the beautiful River Coly. You walk beside it back to Colyton ......and perhaps a cream tea!

WALKING INSTRUCTIONS - From the car park in Dolphin Street, cross the road and walk into the Market Place and cross over to Church Street and walk along this to the road opposite Colyton Cottage, dated 1610. Turn right then left and walk along Sidmouth Road. Take the first road on your left, in 40 yards, "The Butts", and follow it past the houses to a road junction. Here go straight across along Burnards Field Road. This narrow lane soon ends at a gate where you keep ahead on a defined path along the righthand edge of the fields using stiles to gain the Sidmouth Road again. Turn left along it and gently ascend for 50 yards to a track and path sign on your right. Turn right and ascend this track and follow it round to your right to a footpath sign and stile on your left. Turn left and ascend the field on a well defined path to the wooded summit of Sand Hill; the views behind are extensive.

Reach a stile and path sign and turn right on a track and in a few yards right again, as footpath signed. The track immediately becomes a path as you wander through the edge of woodland and in 1/4 mile gain a stile. Descend the field beyond keeping the field boundary on your right to another stile and woodland. The path is well defined as it swings right at first to a stile cut out of a tree. Here it turns left then right to the woods edge which it follows before turning left down to a gate and footpath sign before a road junction. Cross the road and descend as path signed the road to the thatched house - Heathayne. Bear right at the house to reach a ford and stepping stones across the River Coly. Cross these and continue ahead a short distance before turning right and walking towards a bend in the river and onto another before walking beside it to the road on the northern side of Colyton. Turn right then left to the Market Place and back to Dolphin Street and the car park.

Stile cut out of tree trunk.

Heathayne.

44

River Coly - Stepping stones.

Colyton parish church.

COLYTON AND SHUTE HILL - 10 MILES

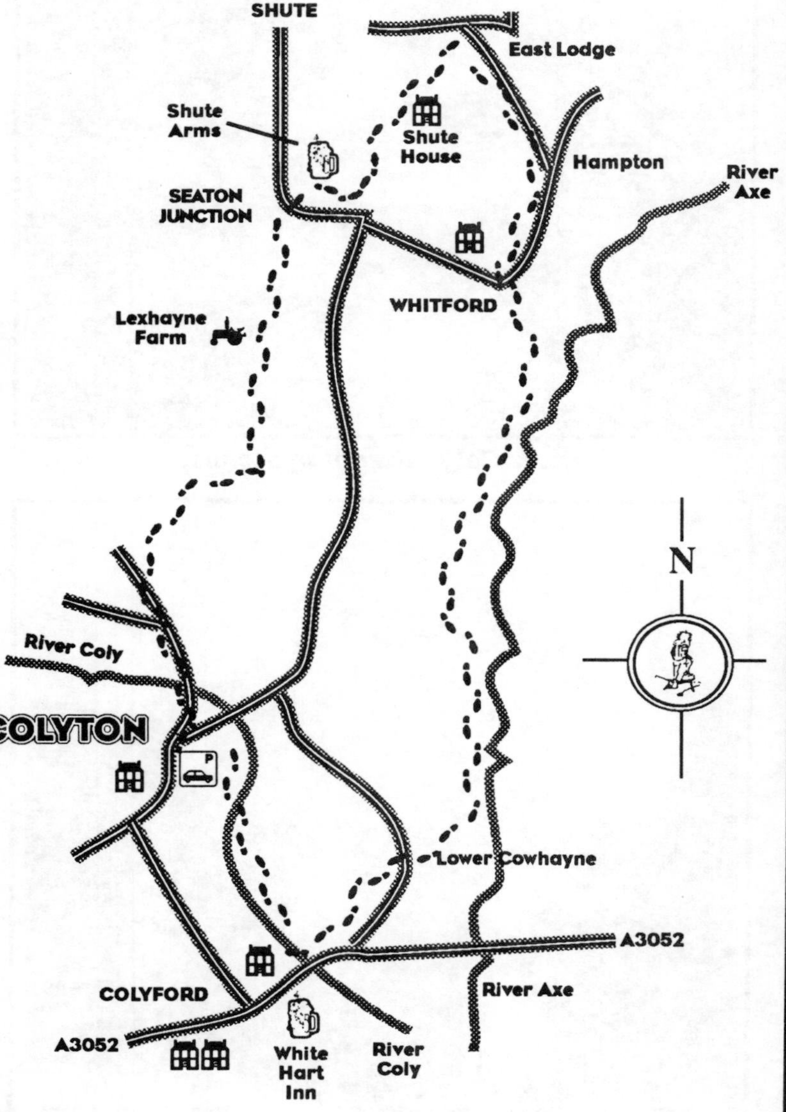

SHUTE

East Lodge

Shute Arms

Shute House

Hampton

River Axe

SEATON JUNCTION

WHITFORD

Lexhayne Farm

N

River Coly

COLYTON

Lower Cowhayne

A3052

COLYFORD

River Axe

A3052

White Hart Inn

River Coly

COLYTON AND SHUTE HILL
- 10 MILES
- allow 4 hours.

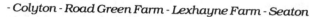 - *Colyton - Road Green Farm - Lexhayne Farm - Seaton Junction - Shute House - East Lodge - Haddon Corner - Hampton - Whitford Bridge - River Axe - Nunford Hole - Lower Cownhayne - Colyford - River Coly - Colyton.*

 - *1:25,000 Pathfinder Series Sheet No. SY 29/39 - Lyme Regis and Axminster.*

 - *off Dolphin Street in Colyton.*

 - *Bear Inn, The Gerrard Arms, Colocombe Castle, Colyton; Shute Arms, Seaton Junction; White Hart Inn, Colyford.*

ABOUT THE WALK - One of the longest in the book but a walk of high character following little used rights of way through attractive scenery. In the Colocombe area I saw numerous grey herons and buzzards flew overhead. Squirrels scampered away in the woodland and a kingfisher flashed by on the River Axe. Shute House is an impressive Georgian building and a magnificent vantage point over the area down the Axe valley. You follow a section of the River Axe and return up the River Coly; the latter being a particularly fine river. You will no doubt see the Seaton Tramway en route and if you have time the village of Colyton is well worth exploring.

WALKING INSTRUCTIONS - Cross the road from the car park and walk into Colyton's Market Place. Descend Vicarage Street to the River Coly and Chantry Bridge. Cross the bridge and keep right along the Umborne road. In a few yards just past Road Green Farm turn right at the gate by the footpath sign. The pathline goes across the field to the bottom where you turn left keeping a small stream on your right. Cross two stiles before gaining another on your right. Cross this and walk along a narrow strip of land with water on either side to another footbridge. Bear diagonally right to a stile and another footbridge under the trees. Cross this and keep the steam on your right to another stile and footbridge beyond. 50 yards later cross another footbridge and bear right to the Lexhayne Farm drive. Gaining it turn left along to the farm where turn right across the field aiming for the large high footbridge over the railway line at Seaton Junction.

Turn right past the Shute Arms and in 120 yards at a T junction turn left through a gate and begin ascending with the hedge on your right. At the top gain a track and continue ascending on this to another gate and stile. Continue ahead a few yards more to a stile on your right. Turn right and descend the field aiming for far left hand corner where there is a stile, reached after crossing a small stream. Enter the left hand edge of the wood and walk up it to another stile. Turn left then right along the drive past Shute House. Follow the drive round for a 1/3 mile to the road at Haddon Corner, just after East Lodge. Turn right then sharp right and follow the lane for 1/2 mile to a road junction. Turn right and walk through the hamlet of Hampton. Continue descending the lane to the road in Whitford more than 1/2 mile away.

In the village turn left and bear right at the next to approach Whitford Bridge over the River Axe. Before the bridge turn right, as footpath signed and begin walking down the Axe valley with the river on your left. The pathline is little trodden but all the stiles are there. In 1/2 mile cross a track from Nunford Dairy by a path sign - Whitford. Continue ahead to a stile with Nunford Hole in the river on your left. Continue to a gate and across the subsequent field with the river well away from you. At the end of the field the river has curved back to you. Just after is a footbridge. Over this you bear diagonally right across the field crossing a ditch to a stile in the hedge. Over this turn left along the field boundary and pass a swampy pond on your left to another stile. Keep the hedge on your right as you curve round to the track from Lower Cownhayne. Follow this to the road and turn left along it to the A3502 road.

Turn right and cross the tramway line into Colyford. Just before the White Hart Inn on your left, turn right, as path signed, and begin walking beside the River Coly. After 1/4 mile pass through a kissing gate and under a pipe before walking round Giles Mill on your left. Don't cross the bridge but continue beside the river on your left for more than 1/4 mile to another footbridge. Over this turn right and soon walk past some houses to gain the road on the eastern side of Colyton village. Turn left then left again to return to Dolphin Street car park.

Shute House.

Typical coastal path stile with dog gate & acorn symbol

SIDBURY & WHITE CROSS
- 6 MILES

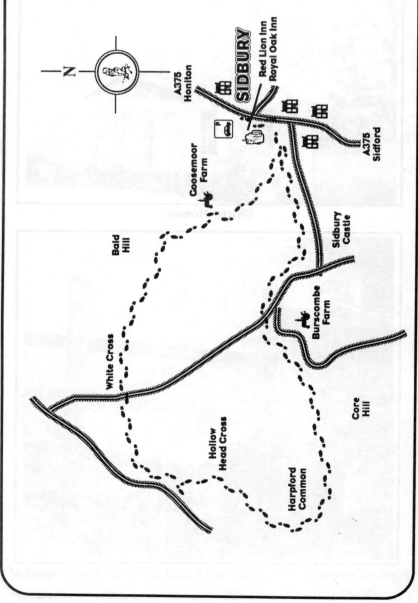

SIDBURY
& WHITE CROSS
- 6 MILES
- allow 2 to 2 1/2 hours.

 — Sidbury - Court House - Goosemoor Farm - Bald Hill - White Cross - Badger's Rest - Hollow Head Cross - Beacon Hill - Harpford Common - Core Hill - Burscombe Farm - Sidbury.

 - 1:25,000 Pathfinder Series Sheet No. SY 09/19 - Ottery St. Mary.

 - Sidbury at Ridgeway Road, Grid Ref.SY138918.

- Red Lion and Royal Oak in Sidbury.

ABOUT THE WALK - Magnificent hilly country with stretches of woodland and extensive views. From White Cross area views to west of the Otter Valley, and impressive vistas from Bald Hill and Harpford Common. The whole walk is on well defined paths and tracks with lane walking at the end back to Sidbury. Enjoyable anytime of the year but especially in the spring when the wild flowers are in abundance. The walk can be joined with the Buckton Hill/Swetcombe, making a very enjoyable long walk around the "hills of Sidbury."

WALKING INSTRUCTIONS - From the car park at Ridgeway Road, return to the main road and turn right along Sidbury's main street, passing the church dedicated to St. Giles on your left, and the Royal Oak and Red Lion inns on your right. Just past these turn right onto the signposted path - White Cross, beside the Court House building. To your left is the Old Bakery. Ascend the track and cross the road to the Manor House, which you will see later, and continue on the track to a gate. Continue on a track keeping the field edge on your right. In its top righthand corner go through a stile and keep the field edge on your left. At the end of this field gain a gate and turn right and follow the track past Goosemoor Farm. Just past the entrance to the farm go through a gate and follow the sunken grass hedged track. Continue ascending for more than 1/4 mile along this track to its end and a stile. Turn right and continue ascending keeping the field hedge on your right and reach a gap in the next hedge. Through this you now ascend more sharply to the ridge of Bald Hill to a stile beside a line of pine trees. Follow this crest to another stile and at the end of the next field another stile and path sign. Bear left to the road at White Cross.

Turn right along the road and in a few yards it turns sharp right; here turn left then right to a gate and follow the descending track to the edge of the wood, where there is a stile. Descend the lefthand edge of the field to a stile, pathsign and minor road. Turn left and follow the lane for 1/4 mile and turn left up the track to Badger's Rest, which is footpath signed. Follow the track past the house and continue up the gate track. At the top where it meets another ascending track, turn left to the cross roads of tracks at Hollow Head Cross. Turn right and follow the level path through Fire Beacon Plantation. In less than 1/4 mile you emerge into the open and take the lefthand track over Beacon Hill and Harpford Common. Follow the track down the otherside of heather plateau and turn left onto another track which descends gradually to the base of the common. Where the track turns right keep straight ahead on a path and for the next 1/3 mile keep to this path - sometimes faint - along the edge of the common, keeping the boundary fence on your right. Reach a stile and cross it and emerge into an open field. Continue straight ahead to a stile 120 yards away, by a path sign.

Turn left on a lane and in a few yards turn right onto a track and back into woodland. Follow this for 200 yards to where it curves sharply left. Here leave it and ascend the "ridge" of Core Hill and descend straight down the otherside to a stile. Leaving the wood behind continue descending to a stile and lane junction. Turn right then left and descend the lane through Burscombe Farm and continue the otherside ascending the lane to a junction. Here turn right then left and follow the signed lane back to Sidbury. You reach the village in 3/4 mile and the main road beside the war memorial on your right. Turn left and follow the road round to the Court House and retrace your steps back to the car park.

OBSTRUCTION OF RIGHT OF WAY

Description of Right of Way
(e,g, "Footpath from Sidmouth to Ladram Bay")

_____
_____
_____

Nature of Obstruction
(e.g. Locked gate, barbed wire across path etc.,)

_____
_____

Location of Obstruction
(Give Grid Reference if possible.)

_____
_____

Date of discovery of obstruction

_____

Name and address of person making report -

_____
_____
_____
_____

Send to -   - you may photocopy this form -

the local Rambler's Association
Footpath officer
or
The Footpath Inspector,
East Devon District Council,
Knowle, Sidmouth, Devon, EX10 8HL

BROADHEMBURY & NORTH HILL - 6 MILES

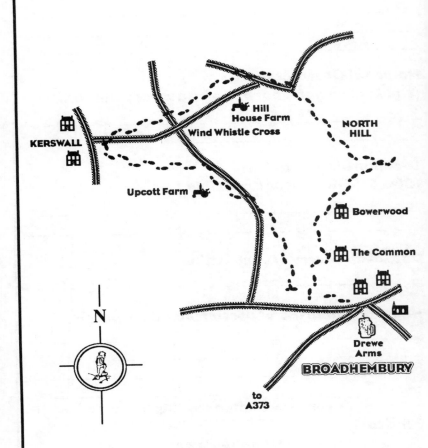

BROADHEMBURY
& NORTH HILL
- 6 MILES

- allow 2 hours.

- Broadhembury - The Common - Bowerwood - North Hill - Broad Road - Hill House - Wind Whistle Cross - Kerswell - Upcott Farm - Broadhembury.

1:25,000 Pathfinder Series Sheet No. 1296 (ST 00/10) - Honiton and Cullompton.

- No official one in Broadhembury.

- The Drewe Arms, Broadhembury at the start/end of walk.

ABOUT THE WALK - Broadhembury is a particularly attractive thatched village and well worth a wander round after the walk. You ascend from the village to North Hill where the Devon and Somerset Gliding Club have their base. The view from here is exceptional over East Devon.You descend a lane to the hamlet of Kerswell before walking across the fields back to Broadhembury and its magnificent church.

WALKING INSTRUCTIONS - Walk down the main street past the thatched houses, Drewe Arms, and Post Office. At the bottom cross the road bridge over the infant River Tale - there is a ford on your right. Turn right immediately and walk along the "No Through Road" around the playing field on your left and a little later "Tower View" on your right. Just after on your left is a stile and footpath sign. Turn left over the stile and ascend the field; open at first then beside the field boundary on your left, as you aim for the lefthand side of Bowerwood. Here is a gate and track beyond. Walk along this to a stile and footpath sign. Map wise the right of way now turns sharp right and goes through the edge of a small wood, but on the ground this is not possible. It is best to continue ahead with the field boundary on your left to a gate and track. Turn right and gently ascend this track - a bridleway - and follow it round to your right along the edge of a pine wood, before it ascends through it. Continue ascending passing two gates across the track before reaching open country. Continue ahead to wooden gate posts.

Here on the crest of North Hill turn left keeping the fence on your left as you walk along the perimeter on the Gliding Club's field. Follow round with the pine woodland on your left to a gate. Here descend a short distance before bearing right underneath North Hill to another gate. Here bear right and follow the track back onto the crest of the hill with the Trig Point to your right - 283 metres. Shortly afterwards reach a road - Broad Road - and bridleway sign. Turn left and descend the narrow lane and in 40 yards on your right is a plaque with extensive views to Cullompton. Continue descending the road and bear left along the lane passing Hill House. 1/2 mile later gain Wind Whistle Cross. Continue straight ahead and 1/2 mile later enter the hamlet of Kerswell.

Take the first road on your left and pass several houses and where the road turns right, turn left as footpath signed, and follow the track on the right of "Tahini" house. Follow the track past a house on your right and another to your left. 40 yards later the track bears right and here you gain a stile close to a stone trough. Go straight across the field to another stile and keep the field boundary on your left - a hedge - to another stile. Continue beside the hedge to a gate on your left. Here diagonally ascend the field to another gate by a footpath sign. To your right is Upcott Farm.

Turn right along the road passing Upcott Farm entrance on your right and continue along the road for 1/4 mile to where it turns sharp right. Here on the corner is a footpath sign, stile and steps. Ascend to the stile and cross the field aiming for the righthand side of a small wood where there is a gate. The pathline in the next field is indistinct but ahead can be seen Broadhembury's church tower and aim for the right of it as you cross the open field to a field corner. Here on the corner is a stile. Cross this and keep the field boundary - hedge - on your left as you descend to another stile and track. A few yards later reach the road and path sign and Bridge House. Turn left and a minute later reach the bridge you crossed at the start and walk back up the main street of Broadhembury.

BROADHEMBURY - An outstanding thatched village - most of the houses are thatched - and is the finest example in Devon. The church built of local stone dates from the 14th century. The Priest House is 15th cntury and the Drewe Arms was originally the Church House.

Thatched cottages at Broadhembury.

Thatched cottages at Sidbury.

RIVER OTTER AND OTTERY ST. MARY - 5 MILES

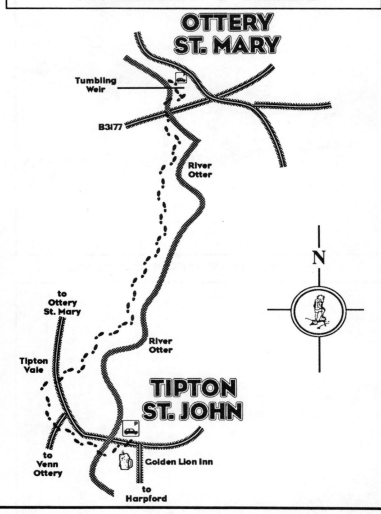

OTTERY ST. MARY - The church dates from 1061 but is mostly 14th century. Cromwell was here in 1645 demanding money for his Civil War. The poet Coleridge was born here and wrote a *"Sonnet to the River Otter"*. Corn was ground at the mill fed by a mill stream dating back to Saxon times. The unique tumbling weir was built in 1790 to power the new four story Georgian serge factory, built in 1788.

RIVER OTTER AND OTTERY ST. MARY
- 5 MILES
- allow 2 hours.

 - Tipton St. John - Tipton Vale - River Otter - Ottery St. Mary.

 - 1:25,000 Pathfinder Series Sheet No. SY09/19 - Ottery St. Mary.

 - Beside River Otter at Tipton St. John. Large car park at Ottery St. Mary, just off Canaan Way.

- Golden Lion Inn, Tipton St. John. Several in Ottery St. Mary.

ABOUT THE WALK - My original plan was to walk up the west side of the river to Ottery St. Mary and return down the eastern side. Regrettably the rights of way down the eastern side are not easy to find or follow, so you have to return down the western side. The walk is particularly attractive beside the River Otter and I have often seen kingfishers here as well as numerous grey herons; trout linger in the water. Ottery St. Mary is a very attractive town and well worth exploring to see the church, historic buildings and tumbling weir.

WALKING INSTRUCTIONS - From the car park on the west side of Tipton St. John, turn left over the road bridge over the River Otter. In 1/4 mile turn right along the minor road to Ottery St. Mary passing the church to St. John the Evangelist on your left. Pass a road junction on your left and at the end of the houses on your left, turn right through a gate and walk along the field edge to a footbridge and River Otter. Bear left to a gate and former railway bridge. You now basically head northwards keeping the river on your right. The path is defined and well stiled, with several footbridges. Sometimes you are close to the river, other times a little away from it. After more than a mile the path leaves the river cutting off a large bend in it as your cross a field to a stile on the right of the former railway line. You now keep closer to the river and in 1/2 mile reach the road bridge on the outskirts of Ottery St. Mary. Cross it and immediately turn left at a gate and continue with the river on your left. You will soon come to the tumbling weir and just beyond is the large car park. To your right is the town. Return the same way back to Tipton St. John; heading southwards and the river on your left - how different everything looks!

WOODBURY COMMON
- 4 MILES

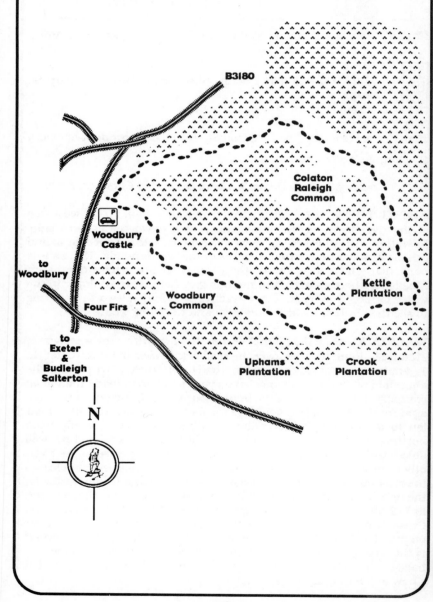

WOODBURY COMMON
- 4 MILES
- allow 1 1/2 hours.

- Woodbury Castle - Woodbury Common - Kettle Plantation - Colaton Raleigh Common - Woodbury Castle.

 - 1:25,000 Pathfinder Series Sheet No. SY08/18 - Sidmouth

 - Beside Woodbury Castle at Grid Ref. 033875.

 - None on the walk. Nearest at Woodbury 1 1/2 miles away.

ABOUT THE WALK - Woodbury Common is superb walking; full of paths and tracks with views to the sea and estuary. The routes are endless and this short walk encircles a small section of the common. The walk is done in an anti-clockwise direction.

WALKING INSTRUCTIONS - Leave the car park by the righthand side and walk along the defined path through the beech trees with the wooded mounds of Woodbury Castle - a hill fort - on your right. Continue on beside the beech trees and in 1/4 mile from the car park the track bears right, leaving the trees behind. About 200 yards later turn left along the track and begin descending the common to some pine trees 1/2 mile away. Where the track forks keep to the left one beside the woodland on your left. Just after turn left by oak trees and follow a track that slowly descends with a small stream to your left. In less than 1/2 mile reach a gate and track. Turn left to a ford and footbridges. Cross these and keep ahead on a track first past pine trees then oak and begin ascending. Keep on the distinct track past an army post as you cross Colaton Raleigh Common. 1/4 mile later take the left track and head for a small cluster of pine trees more than 1/4 mile away. Here turn left on a footpath, which later becomes a track as you curve round back to Woodbury Castle.

WALK RECORD CHART

Date walked -

COASTAL WALKS -

Axmouth to Lyme Regis - 7 1/2 miles ....

Beer & Hooken Cliffs - 7 miles ....

Branscombe and Weston Combe - 9 miles ....

Sidmouth & Salcombe Regis - 6 miles...............................

Bulverton Hill, River Otter & Ladram Bay - 9 miles ....

Budleigh Salterton & Ladram Bay - 10 miles ....

Budleigh Salterton & Exmouth - 4, 5 & 8 miles ....

The Exeter Canal - 5 1/2 miles ....

INLAND WALKS -

Colyton & Colyford - 1 1/2 miles ....

Colyton & Sand Pit Hill - 4 miles ....

Colyton & Shute Hill - 10 miles ....

Sidbury & White Cross - 6 miles ....

Broadhembury & North Hill - 6 miles ....

River Otter and Ottery St. Mary - 5 miles ....

Woodbury Common - 4 miles ....

THE JOHN MERRILL WALK BADGE

Complete six of the walks in this book and get the above special walk badge. Badges are a black cloth with walking man embroidered in four colours on a blue cloth and measure - 3 1/2" in diameter.

BADGE ORDER FORM

Date and details of walks completed...................................

....

NAME ....

ADDRESS ....

....
Price: £2.50 each including postage, VAT and signed completion certificate. Amount enclosed (Payable to Trail Crest Publications) ..
From: TRAIL CREST PUBLICATIONS Ltd.,
Winster, Matlock, Derbyshire. DE4 2DQ.

✆ Winster (0629) 650454 - 24hr answering service.
FAX: Winster (0629) 650416

************ **YOU MAY PHOTOCOPY THIS FORM** *********
"I'VE DONE A JOHN MERRILL WALK" T SHIRT -
Emerald Green with white lettering and walking man logo. Send £7.00 to Trail Crest Publications stating size required.

EQUIPMENT NOTES
.... some personal thoughts

BOOTS - *preferably with a full leather upper, of medium weight, with a vibram sole. I always add a foam cushioned insole to help cushion the base of my feet.*

SOCKS - *I generally wear two thick pairs as this helps minimise blisters. The inner pair are of loop stitch variety and approximately 80% wool. The outer are a thick rib pair of approximately 80% wool.*

WATERPROOFS - *for general walking I wear a T shirt or cotton shirt with a cotton wind jacket on top. You generate heat as you walk and I prefer to layer my clothes to avoid getting too hot. Depending on the season will dictate how many layers you wear. In soft rain I just use my wind jacket for I know it quickly dries out. In heavy or consistant rain I slip on a neoprene lined gagoule, and although hot and clammy it does keep me reasonably dry. Only in extreme conditions will I don overtrousers, much preferring to get wet and feel comfortable. I never wear gaiters!*

FOOD - *as I walk I carry bars of chocolate, for they provide instant energy and are light to carry. In winter a flask of hot coffee is welcome. I never carry water and find no hardship from not doing so, but this is a personal matter! From experience I find the more I drink the more I want and sweat. You should always carry some extra food such as Kendal Mint Cake, for emergencies.*

RUCKSACKS - *for day walking I use a climbing rucksack of about 40 litre capacity and although it leaves excess space it does mean that the sac is well padded, with an internal frame and padded shoulder straps. Inside apart from the basics for one day I carry gloves, balaclava, spare pullover and a pair of socks.*

MAP & COMPASS - *when I am walking I always have the relevant map - preferably 1:25,000 scale - open in my hand. This enables me to constantly check that I am walking the right way. In case of bad weather I carry a compass, which once mastered gives you complete confidence in thick cloud or mist.*

THE HIKER'S CODE

🌼 **Hike only along marked routes - do not leave the trail.**

🌼 **Use stiles to climb fences; close gates.**

🌼 **Camp only in designated campsites.**

🌼 **Carry a light-weight stove.**

🌼 **Leave the trail cleaner than you found it.**

🌼 **Leave flowers and plants for others to enjoy.**

🌼 **Keep dogs on a leash.**

🌼 **Protect and do not disturb wildlife.**

🌼 **Use the trail at your own risk.**

🌼 **Leave only your thanks and footprints - take nothing but photographs.**

REMEMBER AND OBSERVE THE COUNTRY CODE

Enjoy the countryside and respect its life and work.

Guard against all risk of fire.

Fasten all gates.

Keep your dogs under close control.

 Keep to public paths across farmland.

Use gates and stiles to cross fences, hedges and walls.

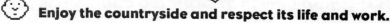 Leave livestock, crops and machinery alone.

 Take your litter home - pack it in; pack it out.

Help to keep all water clean.

Protect wildlife, plants and trees.

STOP Take special care on country roads

 Make no unnecessary noise.

OTHER BOOKS by John N. Merrill Published by TRAIL CREST PUBLICATIONS

CIRCULAR WALK GUIDES -
SHORT CIRCULAR WALKS IN THE PEAK DISTRICT
CIRCULAR WALKS IN WESTERN PEAKLAND
SHORT CIRCULAR WALKS IN THE STAFFORDSHIRE MOORLANDS
SHORT CIRCULAR WALKS - TOWNS & VILLAGES OF THE PEAK DISTRICT
SHORT CIRCULAR WALKS AROUND MATLOCK
SHORT CIRCULAR WALKS IN THE DUKERIES
SHORT CIRCULAR WALKS IN SOUTH YORKSHIRE
SHORT CIRCULAR WALKS IN SOUTH DERBYSHIRE
SHORT CIRCULAR WALKS AROUND BUXTON
SHORT CIRCULAR WALKS IN THE HOPE VALLEY
40 SHORT CIRCULAR WALKS IN THE PEAK DISTRICT
CIRCULAR WALKS ON KINDER & BLEAKLOW
SHORT CIRCULAR WALKS IN SOUTH NOTTINGHAMSHIRE
SHIRT CIRCULAR WALKS IN CHESHIRE
SHORT CIRCULAR WALKS IN WEST YORKSHIRE
CIRCULAR WALKS TO PEAK DISTRICT AIRCRAFT WRECKS by J.Mason
CIRCULAR WALKS IN THE DERBYSHIRE DALES
SHORT CIRCULAR WALKS IN EAST DEVON
SHORT CIRCULAR WALKS AROUND HARROGATE
LONG CIRCULAR WALKS IN THE PEAK DISTRICT
LONG CIRCULAR WALKS IN THE STAFFORDSHIRE MOORLANDS

CANAL WALKS -
VOL I - DERBYSHIRE & NOTTINGHAMSHIRE
VOL 2 - CHESHIRE & STAFFORDSHIRE
VOL 3 - STAFFORDSHIRE
VOL 4 - THE CHESHIRE RING
VOL 5 - LINCOLNSHIRE & NOTTINGHAMSHIRE
VOL 6 - SOUTH YORKSHIRE
VOL 7 - THE TRENT & MERSEY CANAL

JOHN MERRILL DAY CHALLENGE WALKS -
WHITE PEAK CHALLENGE WALK
DARK PEAK CHALLENGE WALK
PEAK DISTRICT END TO END WALKS
STAFFORDSHIRE MOORLANDS CHALLENGE WALK
THE LITTLE JOHN CHALLENGE WALK
YORKSHIRE DALES CHALLENGE WALK
NORTH YORKSHIRE MOORS CHALLENGE WALK
LAKELAND CHALLENGE WALK
THE RUTLAND WATER CHALLENGE WALK
MALVERN HILLS CHALLENGE WALK
THE SALTER'S WAY
THE SNOWDONIA CHALLENGE